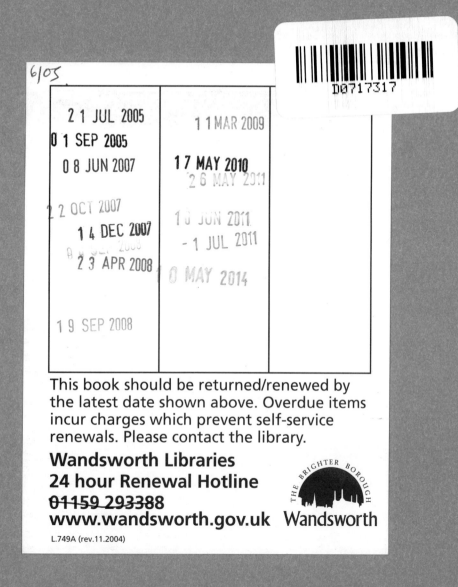

The Life of
St Patrick

Anita Ganeri

H www.heinemann.co.uk/library

Visit our website to find out more information about **Heinemann Library** books.

To order:

☎ Phone 44 (0) 1865 888066

📄 Send a fax to 44 (0) 1865 314091

💻 Visit the Heinemann Bookshop at www.heinemann.co.uk/library to browse our catalogue and order online.

First published in Great Britain by Heinemann Library, Halley Court, Jordan Hill, Oxford OX2 8EJ, part of Harcourt Education.
Heinemann is a registered trademark of Harcourt Education Ltd.

Editorial: Lucy Thunder and Helen Cannons
Design: Richard Parker and Tinstar Design Ltd. (www.tinstar.co.uk)
Illustrations: Mike Lacey
Picture Research: Rebecca Sodergren and Liz Moore
Production: Edward Moore

Originated by Repro Multi-Warna
Printed and bound in China by South China Printing Company
The paper used to print this book comes from sustainable resources.

ISBN 0 431 18083 0
08 07 06 05 04
10 9 8 7 6 5 4 3 2 1

British Library Cataloguing in Publication Data
Anita Ganeri
The Life of St Patrick. – (Life of saints)
270.2'092
A full catalogue record for this book is available from the British Library.

Acknowledgements
The publishers would like to thank the following for permission to reproduce photographs: Alec Holmes **p 6**; Corbis/Richard Cummins **p 23**; Associated Press/Marty Lederhandler **p 26**; Bridgeman Art Archive **p 8**; Collections/Bob Brien **p 21**; Collections/Michael Diggin **pp 12, 16**; Collections/Alain Le Garsmeur **p 17**; Collections/Roger O'Farrell **pp 18, 25**; Corbis/Yann Arthus-Bertrand **p 14**; Mary Evans Picture Library **p 22**; Topham Picturepoint **p 20**; Topham Picturepoint/Press Association **p 27**; Trip/R. Drury **p 10**; Trip/G. Lawrence **p 15**; Trip/K. McLaren **p 24**; Trip/H. Rogers **pp 4, 5**.

Cover photograph of St Patrick, in an illustration of unknown origin, reproduced with permission of Mary Evans Picture Library.

The publishers would like to thank Fr. Martin Ganeri OP for his assistance in the preparation of this book.

Every effort has been made to contact copyright holders of any material reproduced in this book. Any omissions will be rectified in subsequent printings if notice is given to the publishers.

Contents

Words shown in the text in bold, **like this**, are explained in the glossary.

What is a saint?

In the **Christian** religion, people try to live a **holy** life. Some men and women are especially holy. The Christian Church calls them saints. Christians believe that saints are very close to God.

Some Christians pray to the saints to help them.

Some saints look after a country or a group of people, such as doctors or travellers. They are called **patron saints**. This book is about St Patrick, the patron saint of Ireland.

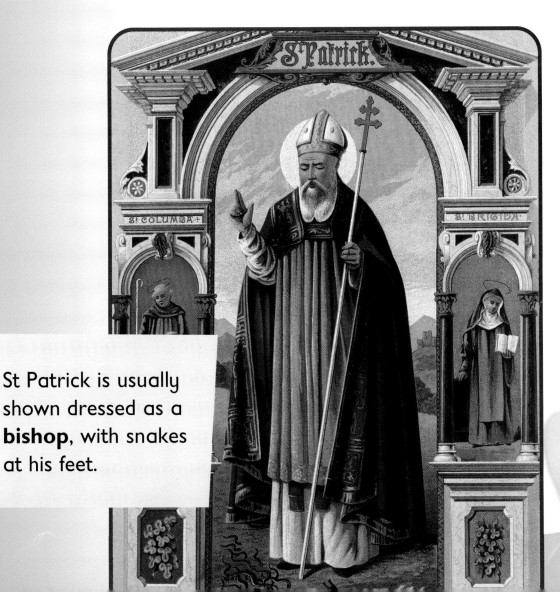

St Patrick is usually shown dressed as a **bishop**, with snakes at his feet.

St Patrick's early life

Patrick was probably born in northern Britain about 1600 years ago. We do not know much for certain about his life. Most of our information comes from stories and legends.

This is Old Kilpatrick in Scotland. Patrick may have been born here.

At that time, northern Britain was part of the Roman Empire. Patrick came from a wealthy British family. His father, Calpurnius, was a **nobleman**. He was also a **Christian**.

Kidnapped!

When Patrick was sixteen years old, he went to stay at his father's farm in the country. One day, **raiders** from Ireland suddenly burst into the farm. They kidnapped Patrick.

Patrick's father was wealthy. His farm would have looked something like this.

Patrick was terrified. He could not escape. The raiders threw him into a boat and sailed off to Ireland with him. There, they sold Patrick as a **slave**.

Life as a slave

A local **chief** bought Patrick from the **slave** market. He put him to work looking after his large flock of sheep. For six years, Patrick worked very hard.

This is County Mayo in Ireland, where Patrick looked after the chief's sheep.

Patrick was scared and lonely. His missed his home and his family. He prayed to God to help him. Sometimes he said as many as a hundred prayers a day.

Escape to safety

One night, Patrick heard God's voice in a dream. God told him that a ship was waiting for him so he could escape. Patrick ran to the sea and found the ship, ready to set sail.

Patrick may have found the ship in this bay in County Mayo.

The ship's captain agreed to take Patrick with him. It was a long, stormy journey. At last, they reached Britain. Patrick was overjoyed to see his family again.

A holy life

Sometime later, Patrick had another dream. He heard a voice asking him to go back to Ireland to teach people about being a **Christian**. Patrick's family begged him not to leave.

Before going back to Ireland, Patrick studied at a monastery in France, like this one.

Patrick had made up his mind – he wanted to become a **monk**. First, he went to France to study in a **monastery**. Then he went to Ireland where he became a **bishop**.

This is a statue of Patrick in his bishop's robes.

Back to Ireland

When Patrick returned to Ireland, he travelled all over the country. He built many churches and **monasteries**. Many people became **Christians** after hearing Patrick teach.

Patrick sailed back to Ireland. He returned to teach people about God.

Patrick wanted to build a great **cathedral**. One day, he saw a beautiful deer and her **fawn** on a hill top. This is the spot he picked for his cathedral.

This is St Patrick's Cathedral in Armagh, Ireland.

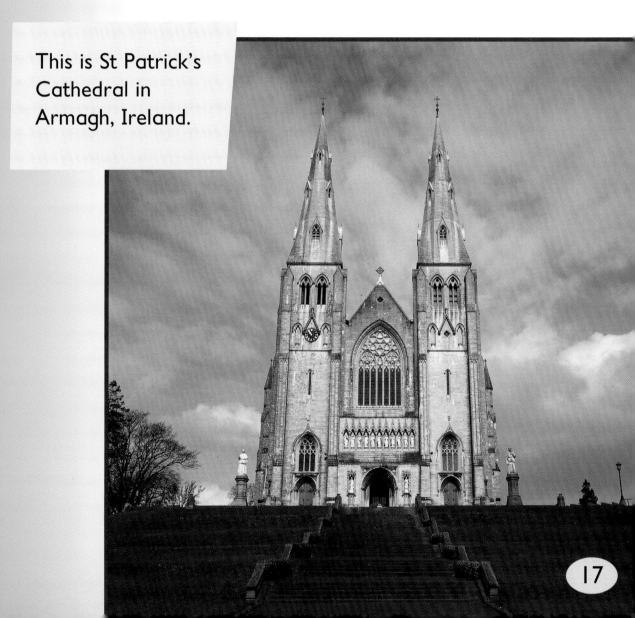

A dangerous life

Patrick's life was often in danger. His enemies, the **Druids**, did not like his teaching about God. One **Easter**, Patrick went to the castle of Tara for a great Druid feast.

This is where the castle of Tara stood. Many chiefs of Tara became **Christians** and followed Patrick.

It was usual for the king to light the first bonfire. Patrick, however, lit his own Easter fire. The angry Druids tried to kill him but he managed to escape.

Patrick dies

Patrick lived a strict life of prayer and teaching. On his travels, he liked to find peaceful places to say his prayers. He especially liked mountains and lakes.

Patrick loved peaceful places like this. This is Croagh Patrick in County Mayo, named after Patrick.

When he was about 72 years old, Patrick died. Legend says that his body shone with a heavenly light. People think that Patrick was buried at a place called Saul in Downpatrick.

Saul was the place where Patrick built his first church in Ireland. This church stands where it once stood.

A snakey story

There are many stories about Patrick's life. One of the most famous tells how Patrick got rid of all the snakes in Ireland. He drove them into the sea.

Patrick is shown here driving the snakes into the sea.

Another story tells how Patrick turned the snakes into stone. In fact, no snakes lived in Ireland. The snakes are probably meant to show people who were not **Christians**.

There are many images of snakes with St Patrick, like in this stained-glass window.

Patrick of Ireland

By the time of Patrick's death, many Irish people had become **Christians**. Some time later, Patrick was chosen as Ireland's **patron saint**. Many churches were named after him.

An ancient cross was put up in honour of St Patrick in County Tipperary, Ireland.

Legend says that Patrick used a **shamrock** to teach people about God. The shamrock has three leaves and each leaf stood for one way of thinking about God.

The shamrock is a very important plant in Ireland.

St Patrick's Day

On 17 March, people all over the world celebrate St Patrick's Day. This was the day on which Patrick died. In Ireland, it is a very happy day with no work or school.

St Patrick's Day is celebrated at St Patrick's **Cathedral** in New York, USA.

To celebrate St Patrick's Day, there are great parades through the streets. There are lots of parties and Irish dancing. People wear **shamrocks** pinned to their clothes.

A St Patrick's Day parade in Dublin, Ireland.

Fact file

- In pictures and statues, St Patrick is usually shown dressed as a **bishop**, with wriggling snakes at his feet.

- St Patrick is also the **patron saint** of **engineers**, people who are scared of snakes, poor and needy people and the country of Nigeria.

- Patrick was famous for doing **miracles**. Once, a **chief** drew his sword to kill Patrick, but Patrick turned the chief's arm to stone. The chief later became a **Christian**.

- Each year, many people make a special journey to Croagh Patrick in the mountains of County Mayo in Ireland. This is where St Patrick liked to go to pray.

Timeline

The only facts we know about St Patrick come from a letter and an essay he wrote when he was an old man. They do not give us much information about his life. We do not know for certain when St Patrick was born or died. You can use the dates below as a guide.

- **Around AD 389** Patrick is born in northern Britain
- **Around 405** Patrick is kidnapped and taken to Ireland. He is sold as a **slave**.
- **Around 411** Patrick escapes and goes back to Britain
- **Around 432** Patrick becomes a **monk** and goes back to Ireland. He becomes **Bishop** of Ireland.
- **Around 444** Patrick builds the **Cathedral** of Armagh
- **Around 461** Patrick dies on 17 March
- **Around 600–700** Patrick becomes patron saint of Ireland

Glossary

AD a way of counting dates, starting from the year zero

bishop leader in the Christian Church

cathedral large church

chief leader of a group or family

Christian follower of the teachings of Christ

Druids priests who led the most important religion in Ireland before Christianity arrived there

Easter Christian festival which remembers Jesus's death

engineers people who design and build bridges, tunnels and so on

fawn baby deer

holy to do with God

miracles events which show God's special power

monastery building where monks live

monk man who belongs to a special religious group

nobleman person born into a royal or important family

patron saint saint who has a special link to a country or a group of people

raiders people who invade a place and steal goods or even people

shamrock plant with leaves arranged in threes

slave person who is forced to work for nothing for another person

Find out more

Books

Celebrations!: Christmas, Jennifer Gillis
(Raintree, 2003)

Places of Worship: Catholic Churches,
Clare Richards (Heinemann Library, 1999)

Places of Worship: Protestant Chruches,
Mandy Ross (Heinemann Library, 1999)

Websites

www.kidsdomain.com/holiday/patrick
Information about celebrating St Patrick's
Day, with lots of games to play and cards
and crafts to make.

www.saintpatrickcentre.com
The website of the Saint Patrick Centre in
Downpatrick, Northern Ireland. A brilliant
exhibition telling the story of St Patrick's
life, with lots of things to see and do.

Index

Titles in *The Life of* series include:

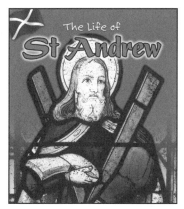

Hardback   0 431 18084 9

Hardback   0 431 18081 4

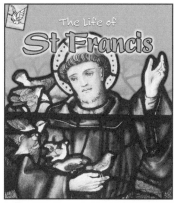

Hardback   0 431 18080 6

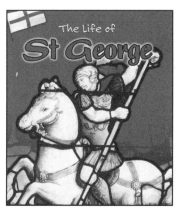

Hardback   0 431 18082 2

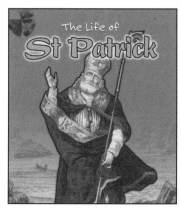

Hardback   0 431 18083 0

Find out about the other titles in this series on our website www.heinemann.co.uk/library